DAFT YORKSHIRE INVENTIONS

Daft Yorkshire Inventions

written by
Ian McMillan

illustrated by
Tony Husband

Dalesman

First published in 2014 by Dalesman
an imprint of
Country Publications Ltd
The Water Mill, Broughton Hall
Skipton, North Yorkshire BD23 3AG
www.dalesman.co.uk

ISBN 978-1-85568-335-8

Typeset in Stone Informal.

Printed in China by WKT

Contents

Introduction

by Keith and Lilian Barnard
Self-styled 'Yorkshire's most inventive couple'

It gives us great pleasure and pride to introduce this book that shows the width and depth and breadth of Yorkshire Inventiveness. Keith wrote that sentence because he's the more practical of the two of us; I'd just say that this book is full of the romance of the inventor, that sudden spark, that Eureka moment, that epiphany, that serendipity.

Yes, Lilian, that's just the kind of thing you would say. You think that by having your head in the clouds, ideas will fall on you like rain, but in the end it's the hard graft in The Inventing Shed that gets you the results.

Yes, Keith, you say that, but remember what happened last time I had my head in the clouds? I came up with the idea for the Methley Cloud Brolly, an umbrella that you would carry when you were in low cloud to stop you getting damp.

Lilian, I've got one word to say to you: lightning. The possibility of strikes. The danger of carrying an umbrella in low cloud as determined by the Ross/Munks Theorem.

That's twenty words, Keith. Anyway, aren't we meant to be introducing this rather splendid book of Inventions?

Yes, Lilian. Have you noticed something?

What, Keith, what?

Lilian, there are none of our inventions in here. Not one. Nowt. I've got one word to say to that: this is disgraceful.

Keith, that's three words. Are you sure?

Haven't you read the book, Lilian?

Of course not, Keith. We're only introducing it.

There are none of our 13,654 inventions in here, Lilian.

What, not the Bingley Envelope for Chicken Sandwiches?

No.

Not the Tingley Self-Trepanning Harness, Keith?

No, Lilian.

Not the Burley Miniature Egg-whisk Cover Holder?

No.

Right then, I'm not introducing their book, Keith. Come on.

At least that's one thing we agree on, Lilian!

Is it, Keith?

Yes!

That's a shame.

The Patent Wallet Clamp

There's nothing a Yorkshireman fears more than losing the money from his wallet and many a time, in darkened pubs in the far reaches of Arkengarthdale, chaps in flat caps will gather to tell horror stories of the time a gale force wind ripped tenners from the wallet of an unsuspecting shepherd who was foolish enough to open it in the market in full view of the weather.

Amateur inventor Seth Butterthwaite of Methley (known to all and sundry as Methley Seth) thought his fortune would be made when, after hours bending over his lathe deep into the night, he perfected his Steel Wallet Clamp which, once affixed, could not be removed

without a quick three turns (one left, two right) of the Steel Wallet Clamp Key.

It so happened that the evening he invented the clamp was a breezy one so he took his wallet to the Dog and Duck to test it out; he affixed the clamp before he set off and his friends were amused as they looked through the pub windows and saw him triumphantly holding his clamped wallet in the air and grinning.

He ran into the pub and announced 'Nobody will ever lose folding money again!' to ragged cheers from the regulars; their cheers became less ragged when he shouted 'and the drinks are on me!' and he fished in his pocket for the key to the clamp, ready to give three quick turns (one left, two right). And he fished again. And again.

And the key was lost. And Seth never found it. And that was the flaw in the Steel Wallet Clamp: that the key, once lost, meant that the money could never be retrieved. And he went back to the drawing board. And he discovered he'd lost the key to that, too.

The Muffler Muffler

George Longstaffe was a very messy eater; his arms would windmill riotously as he ate his Sunday dinner or had his soup for lunch, and while some of his food flew onto the walls and windows of his Rotherham house, a lot of it ended up in his muffler.

George was also a creature of habit. He believed that if he ever washed his muffler, Rotherham United would never get to the Premier League. So, over the years George's muffler became almost solid with dried broth and gravy and calcified vegetables.

This meant that whenever George turned his head, which he did frequently, being a tennis fan, his muffler made a detritus-based noise

that was somewhere between a squeak, a yodel and a JCB toiling up a slope. George always swore he never noticed it but he drove his wife Doreen mad.

'Will you stop turning your head?' she'd say, and George would say 'I can't, it's Wimbledon Fortnight'; or she'd say 'Can I just chuck your muffler in the wash?' and he'd reply, with a catch in his voice, 'But I really want to watch the Millers play Chelsea in the Premier League one day'; and she didn't have the heart to rip it from his neck and fling it into the machine's gaping maw.

So Doreen, being a creative thinker, fashioned a kind of plastic collar that went round the muffler, thus masking the noise and keeping it to a minimum. She called it her Muffler Muffler and, to her surprise and delight, George never minded that when the Muffler Muffler got covered in food-garbage, she washed it.

It was the best of all possible worlds. A home win, as George might say, if you could hear him over the muffler's grumbling.

Here Buy Gum

In a dusty corner of the World Vending Machine Museum in Brownville, Maryland, you'll find the only VM (as aficionados call them) ever invented in Yorkshire, and it was a visit to America in 1959 that convinced Connie McConnell of Holmfirth that the people of the White Rose County would like to buy their chewing gum from a machine.

Connie liked chewing gum, and in the 1950s in Yorkshire she was often frustrated by the fact that because shops closed so early, when she'd run out of gum she had to wait until the next morning to get her sticky fix.

When on a trip to see her cousin Ralph in

New York, she was dazzled by the vending machines on display; in those days they looked like something from science-fiction films. Connie would spend all her loose change on buying bottles of Coke from the machines, and she'd whoop with delight when the bottles plopped out.

When she got home she spent hours in her shed with a blowtorch and some rivets, converting an old dustbin into the world's first Coal Powered Chewing Gum Vending Machine. As if that wasn't enough, she came up with one of the best titles ever conferred on a vending machine: Here Buy Gum. Genius.

Sadly, the Here Buy Gum machine never really took off because the gum would actually gum up the works, and a prototype bubble-gum dispensing machine could not be prevented from blowing the bubbles to enormous size before they were actually dispensed.

Still, there's a corner of Maryland that's forever Holmfirth.

The Cloak of Invisibility

Ladies and gentlemen, gather round, come closer, come closer. You, sir, come closer. Madam: bring the family right up to the stall, I promise I won't bite. Now, let me introduce you to the wonder of the age, the Barnsley Cloak of Invisibilty! Play jokes on your friends! Slip into work late but unnoticed! Put it on and score the winning goal!

I present to you: the Barnsley, er ...hang on. The Barnsley ...hold on a minute. I put it down somewhere. It's not far away. I present to you ...no, that's not it. Everybody stand very still. Very still indeed. The Barnsley Cloak of Invisibility is a marvel but it's fragile. Quite fragile. Stand very still. I'll just crawl across the floor and try to detect it with my fingertips ...

A Sonnet in Praise of Yorkshire Inventions

by Tobias Broom-Broom, 1892

These rolling hills and these boundless dales

Brim with inventors with vast, massive brains

Those paragons of learning, those bright alpha
  males

Who can think of a gadget to unblock your
  drains

Invent an unrazor to unshave your moustache

Or something to tighten your corset without

Recourse to a pulley. These clever men dash

through the Wolds and the people all shout

'Here come the inventors! Some say they're daft

from this point lad tha' can
see hundreds of Yorkshire
inventors inventing Yorkshire things

But we know they're eccentric.' Not quite the
same thing,

But some work with instinct and some with
hard graft

But let's raise our voices and stand up and sing:

Here come the inventors, true Yorkshiremen, all!

When stuff needs inventing they answer the
call!

The Self-mixing Yorkshire Pudding

1. Remove the SELFIE from the wrapper.

2. Place in the Yorkshire Centrifuge.

3. Activate the Yorkshire Centrifuge by pulling the Leyburn Lanyard.

4. Stand well back, in another room if possible.

(Do not worry about the noise of the Yorkshire Centrifuge; it has been described variously as 'The Extinction of the Dinosaurs', 'A Fire in a Tuba Shop' and 'A Very Small War'. It is simply doing its job.)

5. After sixteen hours, turn off the Yorkshire Centrifuge using the Settle Switch.

6. Leave the mixture for three days.

7. Open the SELFIE and enjoy your SELF-MIXED YORKSHIRE PUDDINGS!

Malham man seeks fortune in that London

MALHAM today bids a fond farewell to Adrian Cusworth, 21, who is going to That London to make his fortune as an inventor. "It's the place to be for entrepreneurs and that like," he told our reporter, "and as an inventor myself I feel sure that after a few days down there them money folk will be beating a path to my door sort of thing."

When asked if there was a particular invention he was going to make his money from Adrian pointed at the electronic device he called his MalNav; "It's sort of like a SatNav but for Malham," he explained, "yer can

sort of find out anywhere you want using this as long as it's in Malham."

When our reporter pointed out that London wasn't Malham, Adrian laughed in a derisory fashion. "Of course London's Malham," he chortled, "Where else could it be?"

T' Wheel

In 1926, archaeologists investigating the ancient cave system near Heptonstall were amazed and delighted to discover what appeared to be primitive cave paintings dating from, to use an accurate term, The Dawn of Time.

As well as showing Cro-Magnon Yorkshire Folk indulging in such timeless pastimes as Dwile-Flonking, Knurr and Spell and Ferret Racing, one of the images appeared to show a man in a loin cloth and flat cap carving a round, disc-like object from stone.

Using scientific dating techniques involving rubber bands and hacksaws, the archaeologists concluded that this must be the first example of a wheel and that the wheel, the basis of much of civilisation, was invented in Yorkshire.

A couple of weeks later, with great excitement, the archaeologists returned to the caves, went deeper and deeper in and discovered a series of cave paintings that hadn't seen the light of day. After they'd scraped away the moss and lichen that covered the images, they were disappointed to find that, although the ancient Yorkshire chap had invented the wheel, he hadn't used it for its proper purpose. The paintings showed him using it as a dartboard, a hat, and a plate.

Yorkshire: always first on the scene. Always last to know.

The Aye Detector

As Perkins noted in his *Yorkshire Cyclopedia* of 1863, the best way to tell a Yorkshireman from someone who comes from a minor county is by subjecting them to the 'Aye' test.

As is well known, most authentic Yorkshiremen will utter the word 'Aye' at least three times in an hour; by affixing the Aye Detector, as developed in 1859 by the Steam-Electric Laboratory in Huddersfield, to the chin of the 'Yorkshireman', his Yorkshireness can soon be verified.

According to the Yorkshire Cyclopedia, the people at the Steam-Electric Laboratory were in the process of creating a 'By ...' detector and a T' spotter, but no working examples exist.

THE AYE DETECTOR

How to Invent a Yorkshire Invention

1. Find a Yorkshire-shaped gap in the market for something that hasn't been invented yet. This isn't as easy as it sounds.

A tip: words like Yorkshire Pudding, Parkin, Curd Tart, White Rose, Whippet, Flat Cap and Muffler are useful ones to include in any invention.

2. Make sure that the items you procure for the construction of the invention are reasonably priced if not cheap. This isn't as easy as it sounds. Have you seen how much things are these days?

3. Use a pun-based title for your new invention, to ensure memorability:

Grand Opera Glasses, Champion Flutes, Whippet Cream Whipper, for example.

4. Register your invention with T' Patent Office, which is like The Patent Office except it's in Halifax.

5. Sit back and wait for fame and wealth to accrue.

Electric cap? Steam cap?

FLIPCHART FROM THE YORKSHIRE INVENTORS' IDEAS MEETING

Flat cap
Flat carp
Fat cap
Skipton rope?

Wind driven cap and muffler ensemble?

Sedan chairs for whippets

Own currency:
The How Much?
The Half How Much?

Avoid clichés like the plague

Rother Ham sandwich?

Chairs with Don Castors?

Card games:
Pateley Bridge?
Hebden Bridge?

The Gertrude Fragments

When H L Upton, commonly considered to be Victorian Yorkshire's greatest ever inventor, died in 1901, he left an intriguing sheet of notes addressed to his wife Gertrude. These notes were instructions on how to activate his Time Jar, a seemingly ordinary glass jar which could, in his words, 'transport anyone to any era of Yorkshire past or future'.

Sadly, in the excitement of getting her hands on the instructions after the reading of H L's will, Gertrude tripped and the paper fell into the fire; she fished it out quickly but certain key words and phrases were destroyed by the flames. Scholars have since tried to reconstruct the fragments, but to no avail, so the secret of

Tyke Time Travel remains tantalisingly out of reach. Perhaps you'll be able to work something out for yourself:

THE TIME JAR OPERATING INSTRUCTIONS

Apply the [*words and phrases missing*] to the middle-sized [*word missing*]. Press hard on the [*word missing*] being careful not to [*word or phrase missing*] the [*word missing*].

After [*number missing*] seconds, depress the [*word missing*] being extremely careful not to [*phrases missing*].

Smoke should not [*words missing*] or [*word missing*]. Sounds can be heard, but they should be [*long and complex phrase missing*]. Remember to stand well back in case of [*excitable phrase missing*] or [*apocalyptic phrase missing*].

Do not panic as you reverse or accelerate across the space/time spectrum, unless [*many words and phrases missing here*].

If that happens, run!

GCSE Revision Notes for the Gomersal Thought-Powered Tricycle

Invented by Cedric Walton of High Street, Gomersal, in 1912.

Walton's other inventions included the Goldfish-powered Tricycle and the Onion-powered Tricycle.

Walton was an early member of what would now be called the Green Movement, and his pamphlet 'How the Motor Jalopy Will Take Over the World with Especial Reference to Gomersal' is now a seminal text in the Climate Change debate.

Early prototypes were not successful but Walton insisted he had made the Gomersal 1, an early version of the tricycle, move three inches simply by furrowing his brow and stroking his goatee beard.

Date to note: 5th July 1912, when Gomersal 6, the latest (and last) version of the Gomersal Thought-Powered Tricycle, was going to travel from Gomersal to Wakefield using only the power of the combined thought of the Gomersal Debating Society.

When the tricycle didn't move, Walton swore he would give up inventing, but in fact spent the rest of his life trying to perfect a light-powered unicycle.

Yorkshire Inventions Limerick

There was an inventor from Tong
Whose creations would always go wrong
His planes wouldn't fly
His specs hurt your eye
His glove puppets were fifty feet long.

Muffler Wings

This was a short-lived invention created by a group of academics after the terrible Yorkshire Gales of 1927 when fallen trees blocked roads and railway lines.

John Fleming, a farmer who kept sheep in Swaledale, was struggling to get to his flock when the force of the wind caught his muffler, lifted him several feet in the air and propelled him safely to within sight of his farmhouse.

That night, he wrote to his cousin Alice, who worked at Leeds University in the Aerospace Department, and told her about the incident. Alice told her colleagues and they quickly initiated a series of controlled experiments involving a specially-constructed wind-tunnel, some student volunteers and a number of specially created mufflers. After much trial, error and broken bones a special flying muffler, known as Muffler Wings, was unveiled to the public on June 5th 1927.

Sadly, the muffler wings never really took off, as it were, because John Fleming's muffler had been strengthened by years of him dribbling porridge down it, a factor the scientists forgot to take into account.

THE SUPER TENSILE TEA BAG WASHING LINE

Worried that your teabags will slip from the washing line after you've soaked them for hours and hung them up to dry for the best re-usable quality?

Nervous that you'll have to scrape mud from your re-usable teabags because your washing line's snapped and they've fallen to the floor?

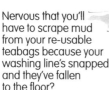

Anxious that, in a high wind, your washing line will snap and fling your teabags into Her Next Door's garden where she'll pick them up and use them as her own?

WELL **FRET NO MORE!**

The new SUPER TENSILE TEABAG WASHING LINE will hold your teabags with a firm grip that doesn't rip the delicate bag thus causing unwanted spillage!

The new SUPER TENSILE TEABAG WASHING LINE has been tested in a wind-tunnel and swung on by Ted Lovell, the OFFICIAL FATTEST MAN IN YORKSHIRE, and it didn't break!

Your cuppa's safe! Kettle on!

Yorkshire Inventors' Club Rules

1. Subs shall be paid weekly. No invented money to be accepted unless approved by the Invented Currency Sub-Committee.

2. Meetings shall be held on Wednesdays, upstairs at the Holmburn Village Club between 7.00-9.30pm.

3. Each member shall bring along an invention each week. This can be at the drawing stage, the working model stage, or the completed invention.

4. Each invention will be tested by the other members of the group and marked accordingly.

5. If steam or electricity or water or batter are involved, suitable protective garb shall be provided by the inventor.

6. If the other members of the club deem the invention to be 'Not Yorkshire Worthy' the inventor shall bear his disappointment with good grace.

7. The disappointed inventor will not shout or aim blows at the other inventors with his fist, hand, foot, knee or elbow.

8. The disappointed inventor will be able to submit another invention for the next meeting, so the disappointed inventor should not sulk.

9. The disappointed inventor must not paint rude words on the walls of the club or let down the chairman's tyres.

10. We all have to be disappointed sometime.

11. Meetings will end with the National Anthem.

Thee Inventions O' Yorksher

by Obadiah Clegg, 1834

Tha can keep thi Wesby-bufflers
And thy cownkern juice is flat
And Hroooo juice might rot thi mufflers
And Riklopopops kill yer cat.

But has tha ivver seen, my friend,
A set of tools like these?
Gorby-saws and Hammerloops
And Nups for climbin' trees

And Quench-Chisels and Nailomatics
And Sleep-by-Claps and Clean-me-Vests
If tha wants an invention that's dramatic
Yorksher inventions are the best!

Lawton's Patent
Atom-splitting Vice Device

Look at the workbench at the back of Keith Lawton's shed. Wait a minute; let me get the torch. There, that's better. Look, there, at the far end. What do you reckon it is? A vice? Well, I'll admit it looks like a vice. Very good.

Look closer. See that jar next to the vice. What do you think's in the jar? No, no, you're wrong. It's not empty. It's full, full to overflowing, actually. What with? I'm glad you asked. Atoms. Tiny little atoms. Careful: don't drop the jar. No, it's not empty. Atoms.

And that's what the vice is for. Keith's going to squeeze the atom until it splits. He's going to split the atom before the Russians or the Americans can do it. With his vice. Don't laugh. He's

serious. Who do you think invented the Jet Engline? Trevor. The ball-point pen? Trevor. The escalator: Trevor.

And that's why we've got to stop him. That's why Lancashire Len has employed us to smash up the vice. Ready? Got your hammer? No, I haven't got the hammer! I thought you'd got the hammer ...

My Dad the Great Inventor

by James Honeysuckle   aged 9

Is tha comin' out?.. lawn needs cuttin' we've lost our James in it'!

My dad is a great inventor
He sits there in his shed
And he think of all sorts of inventions
In the dark and scary and underpopulated
recesses of his head.

He thinks all through the morning
And in the afternoon.
My mam says he should stop thinking and
get some work done
But he says he'll invent something soon.

He writes down all his ideas in a book
That he keeps in a padlocked box
He won't let me or my mam have a peep
or a look
And he keeps the key in one of his socks.

My dad says he will be rich and famous.

The Into Net

Postwoman Martha Topcliffe of Selby had a huge delivery round that involved several isolated hamlets and farmhouses. Sometimes, in bad weather, it would take her hours to trudge and drive to all the places she had to take mail to.

One day she had an idea; she'd open all the letters in the comfort of her house, ring up the people on her round and read the letters to them. Her postbag was too small to accommodate all the opened mail so she got an old net curtain and spread them out on that on the kitchen floor.

The experiment proved so successful that a number of postal delivery workers adopted the practice. Word soon spread, and Martha was

featured on the local, national and international news.

Then two men in suits came to the door; they'd heard about her time-saving/communication project and wanted to hear more about it. Martha was nonplussed when they asked her how it worked. "Well, I just chuck 'em into net," she said.

Into net. A world wide web was born.

Yorkshire Invention Limericks

An inventor called Ivan from Hull
Thought his streetlights exceedingly dull
He created a bright un:
Now when they turn the light on
The glow is both pleasing and full.

Who thought of the rubber milk-float?
Who thought of the self-zipping coat?
It was Mavis from Tong
And she'll always belong
To that place's People of Note.

A flash and a spark and a bang!
Ah, that'll just be Eddie Lang
Inventor of toothapaste:
Too quickly, too much haste.
Now he's just got gums and a fang.

The Child's Book of
Yorkshire Inventions

Look, look. Who is this?
This is Ben. Ben, Ben.
This is Ann. Ann, Ann.

Look, look,
What is Ben doing?
What is Ann doing?

They are hammering.
Hammer, Ben.
Hammer, Ann.

They are sawing.
Saw, Ben.
Saw, Ann.

*They are placing mysterious chemicals
in a bubbling vat.
Place, Ben.
Place, Ann.*

*They are making sparks fly with
electrical devices.
Make, Ben.
Make, Ann.*

*They are running from the exploding
laboratory.
Run, Ben.
Run, Ann.*

*See the laboratory explode.
Bang, bang.
Boom, boom.
Explode, laboratory, explode.*

*What are Ben and Ann doing?
They are going back to something.*

Return, Ben.
Return, Ann.

What are they going back to?
Can you guess?

Ben and Ann are going back to the
drawing board.
Back they go!
Back they go!
Go back, Ben.
Go back, Ann.

Back to the drawing board!
More ideas, Ben.
More ideas, Ann.

Thinking cap on, Ben.
Thinking cap on, Ann.
Think, think,
Think, think
Think think
Think think.

The Full-size Yorkshire Map

Fed up of getting lost when he tried to read maps as his wife drove around the lanes of Yorkshire, Norman Stevens hit upon the idea of the Full-size Yorkshire Map. Norman's wife Janice was an excellent driver and was always exasperated by Norman turning the map and unfolding it and somehow not quite being able to connect the road they were driving on with the line on the map.

Over five long months Norman, using specially strengthened but flexible paper and bottles of multicoloured ink, made a map of Yorkshire that was as big as the county itself. However, the one time they tried to use it was a total disaster as it couldn't fold up small enough to fit into their hatchback.

However, with true Yorkshire fortitude, Norman and Janice can often be seen driving up and down the lanes of their full-size map of Yorkshire which they've now got permanently spread in a series of disused aircraft hangars in Lincolnshire. And Cambridgeshire, actually.

Lump of Coal
Mental Power Organiser

Herbert Naismith worked down Houghton Main pit and was convinced that, somehow, all the world's wisdom was contained in coal. "It stands to reason," he told his mate Keith at the club, "coal is created from millions of years of pressure, millions of condensing atmosphere, trees, plants. It can be made into diamonds. There's got to be a kind of latent wisdom there."

Keith supped his pint and nodded sagely, which was his normal reaction to Herbert's ideas, particularly if Herbert was buying.

Herbert fished out a lump of coal from his pocket. "I've been working on this lump," he said, indicating to Alf the Barman that they'd

have two more of the same, "and I reckon I've invented the world's first coal-based thought transference system."

Keith sighed and hoped the beer would come soon.

"What I'll do," Herbert said, keeping his voice low and conspiratorial, "is hold the lump of coal to my head and transfer a number to your head via the Thought Transference Lump."

A bystander would have found it a tragic-comic sight: two middle-aged men leaning towards each other, one holding a lump of coal to his forehead and grunting. After a while Herbert nodded enquiringly. There was a pause, during which the bingo machine was hauled out into the middle of the club.

Keith smiled and said, "92."

There was another pause.

"Must have brought the wrong lump of coal," Herbert said.

Telegrams from Heston Watts, Yorkshire Inventor, to his Wife

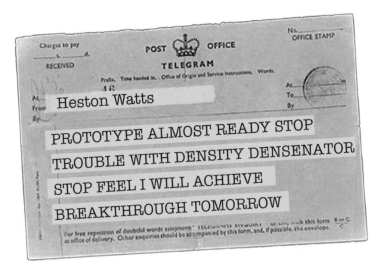

POST OFFICE

TELEGRAM

Heston Watts

PROTOTYPE ALMOST READY STOP

TROUBLE WITH DENSITY DENSENATOR

STOP FEEL I WILL ACHIEVE

BREAKTHROUGH TOMORROW

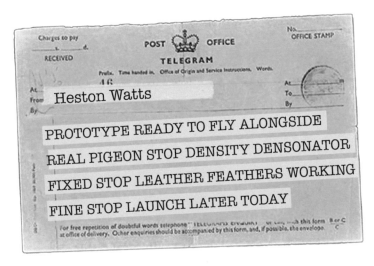

POST OFFICE TELEGRAM

From: Heston Watts

PROTOTYPE READY TO FLY ALONGSIDE REAL PIGEON STOP DENSITY DENSONATOR FIXED STOP LEATHER FEATHERS WORKING FINE STOP LAUNCH LATER TODAY

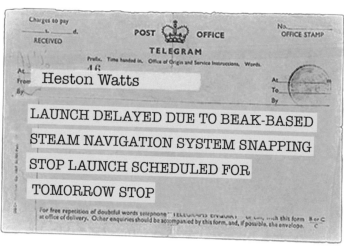

POST OFFICE TELEGRAM

From: Heston Watts

LAUNCH DELAYED DUE TO BEAK-BASED STEAM NAVIGATION SYSTEM SNAPPING STOP LAUNCH SCHEDULED FOR TOMORROW STOP

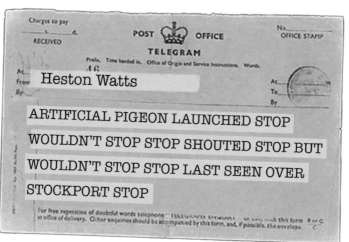

ARTIFICIAL PIGEON LAUNCHED STOP WOULDN'T STOP STOP SHOUTED STOP BUT WOULDN'T STOP STOP LAST SEEN OVER STOCKPORT STOP

Advertising Copy for Failed Yorkshire Inventions

I can send faxes whenever I want with the new Hairnet Fax Machine! Is it a hairnet? Is it a fax? The Fax Speak for themselves!

The Barnsley Bungalow Escalator: gets you to the roof of your bungalow quicker than you can say Wetwang High Street!

I know how much parkin I've chomped because I've got the new Parkin Meter!

My Ferret is as happy as Larry once I've sat him on his Ferret Bike; gentle exercise for our Yorkshire animal pals. And who's Larry? Why, he's my other ferret!

Lost? Not anymore! Flat Cap Sat Nav for up hill and down dale!

Lift Yer Feet Up!

In 1936 the *Yorkshire News* ran a competition for readers to invent a machine to get, in their words, 'the lazy menfolk of this great county' to lift their feet up when their wives were doing the Hoovering. (I know, these were very different times.)

As 'Mrs G', interviewed by the newspaper, said, "When ah'm cleeanin' t' flooer ah can nivver get t' mester to lift his gret feet up so I can gerrunder 'em," and so the competition began.

By the closing date, three months later, over eight hundred ideas had been submitted, including a Steam-driven Winch, a Self-lifting Settee, a Trained Leg-lifting Snake and a Trained Leg-lifting Lizard (these were both

submitted by the same reader); there was a device that sucked all the air out of the room, thus making the legs lift to fill the vacuum so that the vacuuming could be done, and a variation on a water cannon (well, okay, it was a water cannon) that propelled the soaking bloke from his seat.

The winner, though, was Dawn Beeston with her Electric Chair. Put simply, the idea was to wire the chair up to the Hoover (please don't try this at home) so that as the Hoover approached the chair heated up, thus propelling the sitter from the seat.

Mrs Beeston won a lifetime supply of dusters (I know, these were different times) and her husband had to be treated for charcoal buttocks at the local hospital. "Well, he wouldn't shift," Dawn said to the waiting media.

The Daft Yorkshire Inventions Alphabet

A is the apple-corer
driven by steam

B's the Big Flat
Cap: helps you
to dream

C is the Cat Satchel
to carry your
puss in

D's The Stress
Muffler you
squeeze when you're
fussin'

E is The Egg
Bagpipes they
sound really good

F is Frog Linctus
that cheers up
your blood

G is for Gordon,
Hull's greatest
inventor

H is for Harold,
he's Gordon's
first mentor

I is for Illness Cream:
cures all your pains

J is for Jingle:
removes house-
hold stains

K is for Kate Smith
of the self-filling
moat

L is for Lightbulbs
that fit on your
coat

M is for Miracle
Powder from
Leeds

N is Notepaper you
grow straight
from seeds

O is for Otley the
home of the
Steam Knife

P is for Peter Smith:
Kate was his
dream wife

Q's for the quality
things they
designed

R's for The Rust
Zapper the best
you can find

S is for Snoods that
fit over your kettles

T is for Teapots
made from cheese
and metals

PRINCE CHARMING TRIES TO EXPLAIN

U is for underwear
that flies to the
moon

V is for vests
that can play
you a tune

W's for Whale
Sandals seen
from afar

X is for Xylophone
Spanners; yes,
that's what they are!

Y's for the Yachts
that are powered
by horse

Z is for zeal: you
need that of
course

The Yorkshire Dialect
Harness and Bit

A ppalled by the way incomers to the White Rose County were mispronouncing and indeed mangling the Yorkshire dialect, husband and wife inventing duo Ron and Maureen Spibey came up with the Yorkshire Dialect Harness and Bib, a device that would be fitted to the face of, say, a southerner, to make them, in Maureen's words, 'speyk reyt'.

Ron and Maureen, being fluent dialect speakers themselves, knew that the essence of the sound of Yorkshire is to tighten the mouth up, to let hardly any air in or out, so that the vowels become sharper and the consonants can sometimes disappear up their own diphthong.

After much trial and error which saw both of

them being treated for faceache at the local faceache clinic they perfected a cast-iron and leather device which wrapped around the cheeks and down to the lips, thus causing the constriction (some would say strangulation) of the speech of the wearer.

Tapes exist of the first voice test for the device and they make fascinating listening. A gentleman from Surrey is heard to say, before he puts on the harness and bit, "Hello, I would like a cup of tea please, my good man," and after donning the device he says, "R8 giz some char cocker". A design triumph, I think you'll agree!

I Wonder …

It's said that the greatest Yorkshire Inventions over the last four hundred years have begun with that simple phrase, 'I wonder …' Here are some choice examples from the published and unpublished memoirs of great inventors:

I wonder what would happen if I mixed Yorkshire Puddings with gunpowder instead of flour …?

I've lost my key. I wonder if I can unlock the door with this parsnip …?

My whippet isn't as fast as it used to be. I wonder if I fastened this tin of dog food to a fishing rod and tied it to its back …?

I wonder how many flat caps I can pile up before I can climb on them to reach the top shelf in my pantry?

I wonder why all nails are sharp? I wonder if a blunt nail would be easier to knock in because it wouldn't splinter the wood so much?

I wonder why the sky is often blue when there are so many other colours of gloss paint available from commercial outlets? I wonder what would happen if I painted the sky a different colour for each day of the week? I wonder if I'd still need a diary?

Walter Frome's
Coin-forging Hammer

As a lad, Walter Frome of Holmfirth used to enjoy the dangerous practice of putting pennies on railway lines just as a train was approaching; the passing engine and carriages would flatten the coin and render the writing on it alien and strange.

Experiencing hard times as an older man, he came up with a novel idea to make his fortune: the Coin-forging Hammer. Walter soldered a pound coin to the head of a sledgehammer and set up a row of pennies on the patio in his back yard. His theory was, he told police later in a statement, that if he hammered the penny hard enough the imprint of the pound would remain on it.

Sadly the first coin he 'pounded' flew up from the patio and broke the window of a passing bus.

The case continues.

Pork Pie Hat

It was so simple, it was so devastatingly simple, thought Oliver Masson, as he put the finishing touches to his creation. Now the worlds of fashion and cuisine would beat a path to his door. They were laughing before. They wouldn't be laughing soon, or perhaps they'd be laughing at the other side of their crumb-strewn faces.

The Pork Pie Hat. Beautiful. Elegant and sophisticated. The Hat That Is Also A Pork Pie. The Pork Pie That Is Also A Hat. If it's cold, it keeps you warm; if you're hungry, it feeds you.

Oliver tried on his Pork Pie Hat in front of the mirror. A triumph. He walked out into the Bridlington air. A triumph. Above, the seagulls gathered. Prepared to dive …

A Daft Yorkshire
Inventions Acrostic

by Dean Moss, aged 8

Daft Yorkshire Inventions

Are really daft.

Five hundred inventions have been invented,

Twenty on a Tuesday.

Yorkshire is a great place

Or a marvellous place, a

Really marvellous place for

Kids and grown-ups to invent things.

Simon and me invented a

Helicopter made of

Ice cream. It

Rattled when it flew and then melted

Everywhere.

Inventing is good, though, and

Nearly every Yorkshire invention is a

Very useful thing.

Ever wanted a

Nice Umbrella that opened on a

Thursday, whether it was raining or not?

I do. So I invented one.

Okay, it's a bit daft, but I'll

Never get wet on a Thursday because I'm

Smart.

The Pen that Writes Reyt

Janet Butterfield of Finningley, near Don-caster, was upset that, no matter how hard she tried to write her Yorkshire dialect poems down in her notebook, they always came out scattered with apostrophes and weird accumu-lations of letters that, when you read them aloud, seemed to be nothing like the speech she heard on the streets every day.

She decided that the fault must lie with the pen she was using, and, in 1948, began a quest to create a Dialect-writing Pen that would take her the next fifty years to perfect. In 2008, to an astonished press conference of local media, she unveiled her Pen that Writes Reyt.

As the flashbulbs popped she asked a mem-ber of the audience to suggest a line from a

well-known poem; the Opera Critic from the *Barnsley Globe* suggested Wordsworth's 'I wandered lonely as a cloud …' and, to everyone's astonishment, Janet wrote the words on the screen and they appeared as, 'Ah were strolling abart like one of them theer clard things, tha nose'.

Even the hardened hacks in the room shed a tear. It was a magnificent cultural moment.

Essence de Yorksher

The one thing Cyril Watson missed when he moved down south in 1952 was, as he described it, the 'Yorkshire miasma' that followed him around. By this, he didn't mean that he smelled (although some close to him said that he did) but he meant that there was a general smell of Yorkshire that didn't seem to cross the border.

Cyril was a keen amateur chemist and, with the aid of some hessian air-catching bags, he went back to see his sister in Wombwell and set about collecting enough of the local atmosphere to analyse under his airoscope. He took

the bags home to Basingstoke and after several weeks of intensive testing, during which his wife grew increasingly impatient and irritated at the amount of time he was spending in his shed, Cyril emerged with a list of the ingredients to be found in Yorkshire air.

They were: Yorkshire Pudding Mix, Coal Dust, Muffler Microbes, Dialect Detritus and Dry Wit.

"That's what I miss!" Cyril said, on the edge of tears.

"Well, why don't you make something of it?" his wife, a practical woman, said.

And that's what Cyril did. And that's why Cyril and his wife now live in a fifteen-room mansion in Belgravia. His Essence de Yorkshire range of toiletries has been a hit the world over with exiled Yorkshire folk and members of the scattered Tyke diaspora.

And Cyril is still working on new ideas. A scratch-n-sniff flat cap's his latest wheeze…

Walt the Robot Yorkshireman

The noise from Albert's shed is rhythmic, and loud. There's a hammering and a drilling. There's a sawing and a noise that sounds somehow electric. This noise has been going on for weeks, all day and late into the night.

Albert's neighbours have been tolerant, because they know he's a misunderstood genius, but even they are getting to the end of their tether. Secretly, they're getting together a petition to slip under the door of the shed. They like Albert, but there are limits.

Suddenly, on a Friday morning at 11.17, the noise stops. The silence is pure, like the silence you get when a burglar alarm runs out of steam. There is applause from Mrs Green at No 38.

The shed door opens, and Albert appears; well, it looks like Albert but if it's Albert he doesn't look very well. He's walking stiffly; he's clanking as he walks and there's what appears to be steam coming out of his ears. His flat cap seems too big, his muffler too tight, his whippet seems to be a toy one on wheels. The neighbours gather and stare.

Then, amazingly, Albert appears behind what everyone thought was Albert; Albert waves to the watching crowd and shouts "Meet Walt! Meet Walt the Robot Yorkshireman!"

The crowd look puzzled. Albert turns to the robot and says, "Come on, Walt, say something …"

More steam comes from Walt's ears and his mouth opens like a letterbox and he says, scratchily, "Eee gum by. By gum eee. Gum Gum By."

Then, abruptly, his head falls off.

Walt pushes him back into the shed and the hammering begins.

My Day With Daft Yorkshire Inventions

0600: My Flapping Pigeon Wings Alarm Clock wakes me.

0615: I shower, using my Dialect Sooap on a Rooap, that fills my mouth with dialect phrases, making sure I can't speak RP throughout the day.

0630: I eat boiled egg with Yorkshire Pudding Soldiers.

0700: I skate to the bus on my Parkin-powered Skates.

0800: I start work at the Yorkshire Invention Agency. I stare at a blank piece of paper. Nothing springs to mind.

11.00: I have an espresso from my Halifax Mill Chimney Coffee Maker.

11.15: I carry on staring at the blank piece of paper. Nothing springs to mind.

12.00: Dinner time. I press the hooter which makes the noise of a thousand mams calling a thousand Yorkshire kids in for their tea.

13.00: After dinner I carry on staring at the blank piece of paper. Nothing springs to mind.

16.30: I go home on my Magic Steam-powered Carpet in the shape of a Map Of Yorkshire. Another blank day. Nothing sprang to mind.

Diary of Mr Harry Gate, Harrogate's Gentleman Inventor

Monday

Got up. Tried to read ideas I'd scribbled down in the night on my pad. They appeared to say hfhrgudsks. Note to self: invent light that will illuminate my side of the bed and stop Mrs G waking up. Invented fifteen items including Tortoise Pillow Holder and Miniature Stamp-dispensing Submarine.

Tuesday

Got up. Went downstairs. Caught foot in nightshirt and fell over. Note to self: invent Nightshirt Guard, to prevent nightshirt getting caught in foot. Invented 29 items including Picnic

Bagpipes and Steam-powered Goat Milker.

Wednesday

Got up. Banged head on shelf above bed. Note to self: invent wearable crash helmet that does not disturb sleep. Sat for rest of day in Inventing Parlour and invented 41 items including Sandgrain Counter and Trumpet-muffling Gum.

Thursday

Slept in. Woke up at 11.35 because alarm failed to go off. Note to self: invent clock that can be wound by the power of the mind, with simpler models for ordinary people. Invented 53 items including Navel-ink-cup and Household Water Polo Set.

Friday

Got up. Went to Town Hall to receive my Inventor of the Year badge from the mayor. Dazzled by the sunlight bouncing off his chain to the point of bodily incoherence. Note to self: invent non-reflecting gold chain for mayors. Invented 66 items including a Cloud Franchiser and Earwax Combing Kit.

Saturday

Got up, thought it was Sunday. Note to self: invent Self-prodding Calendar. Invented 79 items including Cheese-based Washing-up Liquid and a Staple Gun that also locks your greenhouse door.

Sunday

Got up. Went to church to see how my Electric Pulpit is working and the lights light up. Slight technical hitch: didn't function at all. Note to self: always thoroughly check the prototype before selling it to the church at a vast mark-up. Invented nothing that day. Got to have a bit of a rest. Still, tomorrow's Monday!

Trevor's Turn-up Lanterns

Young Trevor Middleton heard his mother talking about Halloween, one fateful evening in 1962; 'It'll soon be time to make the turnip lanterns,' she said brightly to Trevor's dad who was slumbering on the settee. Trevor's dad snored in agreement.

Because he was listening through the door, and even though the door was of cheap construction, Trevor's mother's words were muffled and Trevor thought she said turnup lanterns.

Trevor was the sort of boy of whom teachers said 'That boy will go far'; they saw him as a kind of wayward genius and they hoped that in the future they'd able to say 'I taught him. I taught that Trevor Middleton'.

Trevor sat in his bedroom with a pair of his

dad's trousers laid out on the workbench under the window. His dad often grumbled when he had to walk down the yard to the outside toilet, so a lantern affixed to the turnups would be a great idea. His mother, Trevor surmised, must have been thinking about Turnup Lanterns too which meant that somehow they were hanging around in the air, waiting to be born. Trevor set to work with an old camping stove and a soldering iron.

Early next morning Trevor substituted the trousers he'd been adapting for the ones his dad was going to wear. The lanterns were affixed, deep in the cavernous turnups. His dad put the trousers on and made his way down to the toilet saying, as he always did, 'I may be some time'.

The rest is part of Wilson Street folklore: the way that Trevor activated the Turnup Lanterns with a remote-control switch, the way the trousers caught fire slowly, the seemingly ecstatic dance that Trevor's dad did, his whoops of 'ME KEX ARE ALEET', the chase down the street involving the wayward genius and the grey-haired man with smouldering clothing.

Hair Restoorer

I attended the address in Growton with WPC Jones, having had reports of a disturbance. I knocked at the door but, upon getting no reply, forced entry using my shoulder and that of WPC Jones.

In the kitchen a middle-aged man was lying on the floor in some distress. A middle-aged woman was shouting incoherently, although I did catch some phrases which I wrote down at the time. These included:

You daft 'aporth;
You're meant to eat it not put in on your head;
Now you look worse than you did before.

As WPC Jones comforted the woman with gin, I attempted to peel what appeared to be a white bathing cap from the man's head. This made him roar in agony. I apologised, which made him roar with sarcasm.

The woman attempted to explain what had happened but both she and WPC Jones had been rendered completely ungrammatical by gin.

I took the decision to call for backup and medical staff attended the man, the woman and WPC Jones. Eventually the man calmed down enough to tell me that he had invented a hair-restorer from Yorkshire Pudding mixture which had been in a hot oven for ten minutes. WPC Jones said he'd been battered, then fell asleep.

Yorkshire Inventor's Insurance

Burnt your fingers in a Yorkshire creative explosion?

Fallen off a ladder in a frenzy of Yorkshire inventiveness?

Got severe headaches from thinking too hard about how the gizmo attaches to the gizmo attachment, in a Yorkshire way?

Your flat cap's caught fire because you were thinking too hard sir... Don't worry, with our insurance cover a new one will be on its way within 24 hours

Done severe damage to your lean-to by placing too many Yorkshire lathes in a space that wasn't designed for Yorkshire lathes?

Well, you need Yorkshire Inventor's Insurance!

For an average of £1.50 a week you'll be fully covered for accidental spillage, droppage, burnage* and collapse.
(Even when you're fully covered with the detritus of the things you've been inventing!)

Just contact Seth Beasley at Yorkshire Inventor's Insurance.

NB: Inventions that are created outside Yorkshire will not be covered. Of course.

*Not the suburb of Manchester.

Yorkshire Inventor's Insurance

Chocolate Teapot

Intrigued by the phrase 'as much use as a Chocolate Teapot', Daft Arnold Pearson decided to make one. He went to Mrs Belshaw's shop and bought half a dozen bars of milk chocolate.

"Ay, what does tha want all that chocolate for, young Daft Arnold Pearson,"she asked, her voice squeaking like a charity shop oboe.

"Ah'm mekkin a chocolate teapot, Mrs Belshaw," said Daft Arnold Pearson, "and I'll bring thee a cup!"

Daft Arnold Pearson skipped back to his house and melted the chocolate in a saucepan. He made a teapot-shaped mould and poured the chocolate over it. The chocolate set and

CHOCOLATE TEAPOT

Daft Arnold Pearson left it to cool. He then carried it round to Mrs Belshaw's shop.

"Get kettle on, Mrs Belshaw!" he shouted. "We're gunner have a cupper!"

As the kettle boiled, Daft Arnold Pearson could hardly contain his excitement. "It'll taste a bit like tea and a bit like chocolate!" he shouted.

Mrs Belshaw was dubious: "Are tha sure it'll not melt and that?" she asked. '

"Hey!" Daft Arnold Pearson replied, "they dun't call me Daft for nowt!"

Multi-storey Car Parkin

Gordon Smallman loved parkin and he loved driving and in 1982 he invented a way of stacking Yorkshire's favourite cake to snack on as he drove, without taking his hands off the steering wheel.

In the past his problem had always been that he had to wait until he stopped at traffic lights or pulled into a layby to eat the parkin. This left him, in the words of his mother, 'grumpy as a cracked drainpipe'.

Using a system of levers and pulleys in the front of his old Ford Anglia he rigged up a multi-layered delivery chute that he was able to operate with his eyebrows. One wiggle of the left eyebrow meant 'Give me parkin'; one

wiggle of the right eyebrow meant 'Give me more parkin'. Two wiggles of the left eyebrow meant 'Hold the parkin for a moment' and two wiggles of the right eyebrow meant 'No, dash it, give me more parkin'.

For several months the system worked well and Gordon became deliriously happy and four stone heavier. Sadly, in January 1983, a wasp flew into the Anglia and landed on Gordon's eyebrows.

Oh, you can guess the rest. Oh, it was horrible. Oh, it was messy. Oh, parkin was involved. Oh, the parkin got everywhere.

Incomprehensible Yorkshire Dialect Description of the Invention of the Steam Clog

1. Seez, tha gets thi gubbinz and flecks it onto t' eal o' t' clog (tha munt get ter gain else tha'll singe thi eead) then efter a bit tha adds thi juis and thi stuff. T' wheels and t' sprokets come next, then t' boiler to mek t' steeam. Boiler'll be stuck to t' clog bi t' gubbinz and t' juis and t' stuff.

2. Stoke thi boiler an' get plenty o' steam guin. Then put t' clogs on. They might be a bit waaarm but dun't panic. Mek sure thaz gorra bucketer watter handy.

3. Then start guin. Tha'll gu! Tha'll gu reyt! Like summat off a shuvvle! Gu! Gu!

It does what it says on the packet... nowt!
THE AUTOMATIC SPRING DEVICE

The Automatic Spring

This invention, by John Threadneedle of Halifax, probably ranks as the daftest of all the Daft Yorkshire Inventions in this book. But then again, probably not, if you've read the rest.

In 1956 the young John heard his mother Doreen complaining that her flowers weren't growing fast enough. As his dad Brian pointed out, that was probably because it wasn't spring yet, but John set to with his exercise book and ruler and a set square (he was a maths-minded lad) and devised something that, as he said to his mother, 'would mek her flowers come sprutting up'.

He made her wait in the house until the device he'd made in his den was ready. He then led her and his dad out into the garden where it appeared that he'd slipped a net over the nascent flowers.

John pressed a button on a primitive electronic device and the net began to gather up the shoots that were just appearing. Doreen was horrified; "What's happening?" she shouted.

"I've stuck a wire in each sprutter and t' elecric'll drag 'em out on t' ground double quick," he said. "It'll be an instant, artificial automatic spring!"

Better luck next year, Doreen!

Afterword

by Jeremiah Gross the Bard of Boar's Head Clough, 1598

Great Yorkfhire Inventionf

Oh Yorkfhire, place of fertile brain
Where planf are made to make the thingf
To melt the fnow, collect the rain
Make potion from a bee'f fharp fting
And give to all the lovely world
A ftick that makef your hair right curled.

Oh Yorkfhire, planf are not enough
You need to bring them to fruition!
From firft idea to actual ftuff
Requiref fkill and graft and erudition;
And that'f where Yorkfhire folk excel:
They make thingf and they make them well!